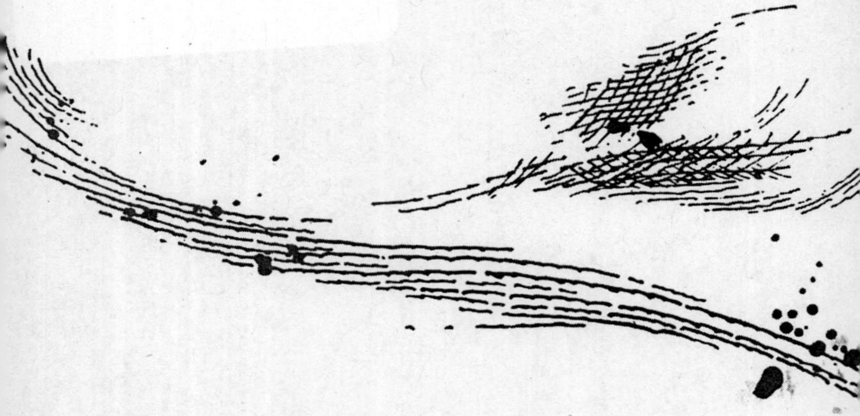

MR ABHIMANYU (A PLAY)

LAKSHMI NARAIN LAL

Translated by SURESH KOHLI

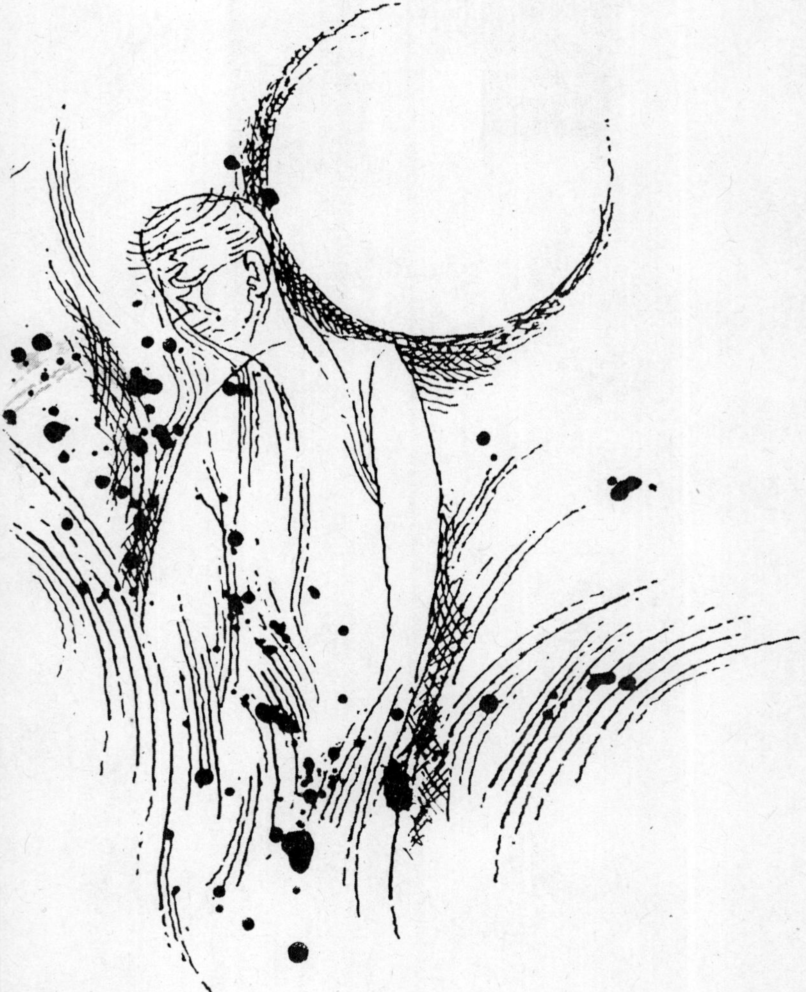

MR ABHIMANYU

MR ABHIMANYU

An English translation of
Dr Lakshmi Narain Lal's Hindi Play

Translated
by
Suresh Kohli

MOTILAL BANARSIDASS
DELHI :: PATNA :: VARANASI

MOTILAL BANARSIDASS
Head Office : BUNGALOW ROAD, JAWAHARNAGAR, DELHI-7
Branch Offices : (i) CHOWK, VARANASI-1 (U.P.)
(ii) ASHOK RAJ PATH, PATNA-4 (BIHAR)

1st Ed. English Translation 1971

Printed in India
BY SHANTILAL JAIN AT SHRI JAINENDRA PRESS, BUNGALOW ROAD, JAWAHARNAGAR, DELHI-7, AND PUBLISHED BY SUNDAR LAL JAIN FOR MOTILAL BANARSIDASS, BUNGALOW ROAD, JAWAHARNAGAR, DELHI-7.

TRANSLATOR'S NOTE

I am indebted to Mr Kanwal Kishan for his assistance and advice which helped me understand the play more profoundly, to Srikant Varma (whose introduction to the Hindi version was a great help), Pawan Tandon for his help in preparing the manuscript. Dr Prabhakar Machwe has been a constant source of inspiration during all this period as his discourses on the plight of modern human beings were a great deal enlightening.

I am grateful to Dr Lakshmi Narain Lal for having given me an opportunity to translate this play, as also for his patience, advice and understanding.

Mr Abhimanyu : Some Stray Thoughts

Man is subject to mutability, "youth grows pale, and spectre-thin, and dies." "There is a space of life between boyhood and maturity (wrote Keats) in which the soul is in a ferment, the characters undecided, the way of life uncertain, the ambition thick-sighted." This is the moment of youthful commitment which when lost or wasted brings a kind of romantic sadness and when later reflected upon brings on romantic nostalgia. When the attitude of mind leads to desires that are impossible to achieve, it becomes destructive and self-defeating. If one is not physically destroyed by such disillusionment, life loses its purpose, and man becomes an eternal wanderer, alienated from society, an outcast and a scapegoat. The central character of the play or the protagonist, Rajan, is blinded by his innocence and has not yet reached the point—the shadow line—where he is aware of the catas-trophe to which frail man is subject, or the evil that exists in others, or the evil that is latent in his own self.

Rajan is a tormented and lonely man, plagued by grief, and wrecked by guilt. He is often in flight from himself, modern-day Abhimanyu, caught up in a trap, whose only crime is his getting into this trap. Towards the end in his encounter with his alter-ego or the destructive element he is morally destroyed, while the alter-ego or the other self has been alienated from the very self—he is physically destroyed. In the end we find he has compromised (unlike the Abhimanyu of the epic times who prefers to die rather than to compromise), has undergone a change; he has peeled away his illusions, abandoned his hopeless dreams of getting out of the system which has entangled his very self, and ultimately accepts himself for what he is and for what he can do in that direction. He accepts a new assignment "whicn was for someone else". Rajan immerses himself in the destructive element, and he is sustained by his dreams at the same time as the dream is tempered by experience.

Rajan is usually misused by others before he is overwhelmed by the passing of time. His decline seems inevitable and fated. Fascinated by the process of deterioration and decline, Dr Lal seems to be wondering about what has happened to Rajan, his character and what he can do to revive him. But can he be revived ? Dr Lal seems to be leaving it to us to ponder over the problem and find an answer. He is leaving it to us not because he is not sure of his grounds or what he wants the modern Abhimanyu to be, he is very sure of that. He is leaving it to us because we are responsible for the degradation and disillusionment of a modern, honest man. Each culture and society is an organism which has a pattern of birth, growth, maturity, and subsequent decay or decline—a belief that eventually everything would return to its perfect state, that it would return to its origin and that the cycle of life would be repeated—the passing of the cultural spring and summer would ultimately come back to the recapitulating winter, having suffered autumn.

Several people have invariably asked me as to why I picked up Dr Lal's *Mr Abhimanyu* for translation, what is there in it for my restless nature? The reason or the answer is very simple. I found the play a great deal aesthetically satisfying. And, as usual, my interpretation of the play differs from those of others including perhaps, Dr Lal himself. To my mind, Dr Lal rejects the attitude that ordinary life is trivial and banal,conventional or mechanical; that men live secondhand, unauthentic lives, rejecting spontaneity; that their lives are not of quiet desperation but of backslapping complacency; that ordinary life has fallen into the quotidian. Dr Lal does not decry that ordinary life is little conducive to human nobility and to a very large extent agrees with De Tocqueville that "the language, the dress, and the daily actions of men in democracies are repugnant to ideal conceptions" that "a modern mass society has no place for such qualities, no vocabulary for them, and no ceremony...which makes them public..." Rajan is unable to end his alienation, although he wants to. Dr Lal feels that if Rajan cannot be a part of society as a whole, can he, at least, be to a part of it ? But Rajan does not find such a part because it is not in him to find it, but he longs for it all the time. Dr Lal's thesis is that a noble or sincere human being is crippled in modern society, he is helpless and has to compromise in-variably because he is reduced to such a situation. As such he goes back and reflects what happened innumerable centuries ago, in the *Mahabharata* when Abhimanyu, son of Arjuna and a nephew of Lord Krishna, is caught up in a military trap and gets lost and is ultimately killed-he knew the way to get in but, alas, he did not know how to come out of it. Rajan is a modern Abhimanyu (beauti-fully suggested through the title of the play) who has innocently got into the trap (the system) and makes a desperate attempt, unsuccessful though, to come out of it. But alas, he cannot !

Dr Lal's concern in the play is not so much with the individuality of Rajan or even the atmosphere in which he lives. His concern is with the system—the social system, the political system and the administrative system—all working simultaneously on a superficial level. There is a serious difference between the Abhimanyu of Vyasa and the Abhimanyu of Dr Lal. Abhimanyu positively wanted to come out and he fought an honest battle for it but he failed and he was killed. On the contrary, Rajan, i.e., *Mr Abhimanyu*, does not want to come out, he has the illusion that he wants to come out. In order to give posi-tivity to his illusion he fights a battle, a battle in the true sense and not a superficial one. The only thing is that it is a battle of an uncertain man, a man in grave doubts. Abhimanyu's victory was in his defeat, while Mr Abhi-manyu's defeat is his defeat: it is the tragedy and insecu-rity of the modern man whose death is not in greatness and whose life is not a determination of courage. In a way, the era of greatness and courage has vanished: now we have only individual or personal battles left to fight out. The battles that cannot be projected through epics but through the depiction of one's own personality and capa-city to decide in wholeness the way one has chosen in an attempt to search for values, values which are very important for the modern man.

Dr Lal's characters are live characters, an integral part of the society which India has built all these years, follow-ing the partition of the country which we innocently call *independence* or *freedom*. The society whose pillars are capitalists like Kajariwal, their political spokesmen or mouthpieces like Gaya Dutt, Rajan's lawyer-father who gives more prominence to social behaviour rather than individuality, Rajan's wife Vimal who is not aware of the moral values, corrupt officials, ministers, the police and above all Rajan himself. Every system is a conspiracy, ultimately. The present-day social system in India is also a conspiracy, such a conspiracy from which one does not see a way to get out but also one can't even live in it because it is suffocating. Rajan's tragedy begins where he gets the realization that he is a part of this great conspiracy. We have thousands of officers, millions of workers and low-paid clerks who in order to fulfil their own selfish motives will go ahead to strangle anyone's neck. They invent new ways but they do not have the realization that they are in the wrong, that they are digging their own graves. In fact, it is part of their inheritance. This is their weapon of defence and this is their conscience. Dr Lal has stated this beautifully during a conversation or confrontation of Rajan with the idealistic labour leader Atman

RAJAN: Mr Atman, educated people like you shouldn't join such dirty politics.

ATMAN: You mean I should have joined the administration?

RAJAN: Well, politics has spoiled even administration.

ATMAN: Red-tapism is all we have learnt from the British. Bureaucracy has vitiated politics too...

RAJAN: Your politics also come from the same system. ATMAN: Well, it all comes from there.

RAJAN: The British are not there any longer? ATMAN: The system remains the same.

RAJAN: Why don't you change the system? You're a popular labour leader; even then you lost to Gaya Dutt. . . .Strange?

And although a part of them all, the same class, Rajan is somewhat different. His career was chosen for him by his father; his vocabulary or phraseology stems from the educational system. His clothes have been chosen by his wife. And,in fact, everything which is his has been chosen by others. There is nothing which he could call his own. There is only one thing which makes him different from others, and that is his *realization*.

In fact, generally this question does not arise in people's life whether they have any ideology or not. They just become a part of the system. But this question arises in Rajan's life in an extraordinary manner. He is told that he has got a promotion which is not due to his own efforts and work, instead, he is informed that this promotion is due to the victory of the official candidate of the ruling party. The man is Gaya Dutt, ill-mannered, uncivilized, a man without any dignity, whom he hates intensely. He is being made a Commissioner from a Collector. He is being made a part of a big conspiracy despite the fact that he is not at all responsible for Gaya Dutt's victory. In other words, he is being trapped into a conspiracy which has already been set into motion. Rajan's conflict starts from this very point but the fight ends very soon. In a vain struggle to fight the system he is defeated by his own self, his own alter-ego. Dr Lal depicts this beautifully through a confrontation of Rajan with his own self, with his own alter-ego :

> How could yo do that, you senseless...having lost, why do you do this drama of struggle ? You have nothing to do with Atman. You had left him the moment you got in here...then I was born. Atman, Gaya Dutt, Rajan, Kajariwal—you have formed a sort of quagmire, a sort of trap around yourself ...I have been fighting all along...The same lost

> battle...I have been working honestly...You have been honestly trying to keep up the system...That was all in my power...Why didn't you come out of it then?...I am a responsible person...Not *person* only responsible (laughter), a talented and sagacious person is special in everything, special even in his service...I have never done any injustice...You only did injustice to yourself...Day and night I was absorbed in my work...But never let yourself into anything. Saved something everytime for this day.
>
> But it never happens, nothing like this happens...

and this dialogue with the self continues until it reaches a point where everything becomes crystal-clear :

> For the safe defence so many arguments, so many principles...How can you say that?...Yes, you did a lot of justice only to hide injustice. You punished the criminals only to hide the crime, to cover the crimes. Committed suicide only to keep yourself alive ... Then you had the idea that after indepen-dence the struggle for freedom starts...That is there even now ... With my birth a new confidence took birth in you. There are only two ideas in modern society: service and politics...

Rajan is materialistic, he wants to resign but he does not; he gets Kajariwal's godown sealed but does not have the courage to overrule the orders; he dislikes the system yet does nothing to break it. He does not want to come out of the system in actuality. Because there are dangers in coming out: inside it is oppressive but still there is a sense of security, while outside there is salvation but there is death too—a death which is both physical and moral. Now it is doubtful whether Rajan really wants to come out of the system. If he does not want to come out, then this revolt is a beautiful instance of showmanship, of pretension. Why does he dislike Gaya Dutt ? Because he is an agent of the capitalists or is it because he is un-cultured ? The main reason for this doubt is Rajan's hatred of politics. If Rajan were against Gaya Dutt's ideology, he would have adopted a different technique, he could have come out of the system in that case. But it is not Rajan but Atman who is against Gaya Dutt's political ideology. It is Atman who is fighting Kajariwal through Gaya Dutt and Rajan. It is Atman's life which is in danger and not that of Rajan. It is Atman who gets killed and not Rajan who stays alive to compromise.

According to Srikant Varma: "In fact, in Atman's end lies Rajan's end. With the use of 'fantasy', Lakshmi Narain Lal has contrived the relationship between Rajan and Atman with competent craftsmanship :

RAJAN: But how about the gap between the step and the ground ?

(*Atman laughs*)

You laugh at that. You don't know me well, do you ?

ATMAN: How could I do that? I joined politics and you came into Administration...You then got busy with your domestic life, worked day and night and I got into the opposition... Saw you a couple of times by the way but you always evaded me. I even waved to you a number of times. A number of times...

Needless to say that Atman is a part of Rajan's self, a part which was thrown aside the day Rajan came into Administration. Gaya Dutt is another part of Rajan. Rajan could have been Atman but Gaya Dutt saw to it that he did not. Atman is killed with Gaya Dutt's revolver but it comes into prominence in Rajan's conscience, in the shape of a murder committed by Rajan.

It would be remarkable to depict a mythological character in a new form in a verified vision but to take into account the real meaning of a mythological character's participation in an action and through that project the com-plexities of the time is much more difficult.

It could be a matter of interpretation and it is very likely that the way I have interpreted the character to myself may be wrong but there are questions that come to my mind which give way to my own doubts and as such to the interpretation of the play. As it is, my only quarrel with Dr Lal is his comparison of the great Abhimanyu of the epic times with a comparatively weak-willed modern Abhimanyu. Is Dr Lal trying to project the transformation of a brave man of the epic times to the present day? To my mind, Dr Lal's Abhimanyu is more like the legendary Trishanku who is hanging up in the air—neither on the earth nor in the heavens—having been rejected by both. To me, Rajan is more like Trishanku because he is neither in the system nor out of it—he is in-between the two, yet a part of none. Mr Virendra Narain who directed the play in Hindi said in his production manual: "Rajan is very vocal and accuses each one of them. One also discerns a note of self-pity and outburst of temper promising a revolt—a breakthrough. Probably he is aware of his destiny. Probably he has guessed the end and the louder his protests, the helpless-ness becomes more pronounced. It is most ruthlessly revealed that the opportunism of Gaya Dutt, the idealism of Atman and the outbursts of Rajan form a distinctive pattern embellished by Mrs Rajan and Mrs Rathor to depict the vacuum which is our life today. The tragedy is not of a fighter losing a battle. The tragedy is of a dead man trying to live and finding himself dead and finished."

Would you call it a tragedy ? Well, we leave it to you.

I do think all that I had to say has been said and it would be better to let the reader study the play in the modern context of modern Indian society and decide for himself who is responsible for the degradation of the modern man...

Suresh Kohli

New Delhi
November 1971

Act One

SCENE ONE

(Setting: The front room of the Collector, Mr Rajan's bungalow; a door in the rear to get in. On the right of the door is an office table, with a typewriter and some papers placed on it, and a few chairs. A little away from this is a small table with a telephone on it.

On the left of the stage are two sofa-sets and a table in the middle with an ash-tray and a newspaper. There is a bookshelf on the wall just behind the sofa-sets. This contains, apart from some books and toys, a flower vase and a broken sculpture-piece made of stone.

For a few seconds, after the fading of lights, a special tune flows in the darkness and breaks when the light falls on Rajan sitting on a sofa, absorbed in a file. Suddenly he gets up, walks to the office-table, glances through a paper or two and then sets his eyes on a paper rolled in the typewriter. He is impatient and in that very state walks to the book-shelf, takes out a book and while unfolding it his eyes catch sight the broken piece of sculpture. A smile appears on his lips. He puts back the book and takes out another. At that moment enters Vimal from the door in the rear.)

VIMAL: Listen !
(Rajan closes the book somewhat abruptly)
It is almost ten now.
(Rajan tears some paper off)
Tell me, should I...
(A musical toy falls down which is picked up by Vimal but Rajan takes it from her and after having shaken it for a while puts it beside the broken piece of sculpture)
What's wrong ?
(He does not speak but picks up the file from the sofa. Vimal starts playing the toy, a mild but strange tune comes out of it. At one point Rajan wants to tear the file off and in a vain struggle to do that he walks into the house. Sri appears on the door at the right)

SRI: Sahib's father is here, madam.

VIMAL: Really ?
(Rajan's father walks in. Vimal touches his feet in the traditional way)

FATHER: Where's Rajan ? I hope all is well.

VIMAL: Why don't you come in ?

FATHER: *(Sits on the sofa)* What's this strange news, Vimal ?

VIMAL: *(Turning to Sri)* Tell Sahib that Father is here.
(Sri goes in)

FATHER: Sit down, Vimal. It's difficult to explain : the moment I reached home from the court I found the manager of Kajariwal Mills waiting for me. And what he told me was baffling. I was happy that Rajan has now become the Commissioner and I had thrown a number of parties for that. I almost staggered, when I heard he was resigning. Tell me why is he doing so ? Do you have any idea ?

VIMAL: I am myself amazed.

(*Sri enters*)

SRI: He is coming.

(*Sri walks out*)

VIMAL: It's good you've come. I was thinking of ringing you up tomorrow.

(*Rajan enters, greets his father with folded hands*) FATHER: Come along, son. What is this rumour... ?

(*Silence for a while*)

RAJAN: You know I have always been opposed to this kind of work... FATHER: That's right.

RAJAN: And I've done what you wanted me to. You had a desire to see your son a Collector or a District Magistrate. Aren't you satisfied now... ?

FATHER: (*Laughter*) It is just the beginning, my son.

RAJAN: What do you mean ?

FATHER: I am talking of a basic thing.

RAJAN: I'm also saying the same. I am getting out of this job. (*Pause*) The minister was here a few days ago.

FATHER: I read that in the newspapers.

RAJAN: Since then I have been mentally disturbed. He told me that the ruling party never ex-pected the victory of the official candidate. He led me to believe that the happy result was due to my efforts. I don't know how that could be. I don't recall to have done anything in that direction. What he meant was that I did some manipulations and indulged in foul-play to get their candidate elected. He congratulated me on my promotion and gave me a hint that this new assignment was a reward for that. Now this is really absurd.

FATHER: How does it matter to you ?

RAJAN: It does.

FATHER: But you are sincere, aren't you ?

RAJAN: No one has the place he deserves. I am obs-tructing someone else's due. This post was for someone else.

(*Pause*)

And you know what the minister said ? He said : "Mr Rajan your work during the election has been commendable. So we are offering you such an important post. You will have to raise at least Rs 12 lakhs for the next general elections."

(*Meanwhile Vimal goes out and comes back with a glass of water for Rajan who is now sitting on the sofa*)

VIMAL: Why don't you come to the living-room, Father ?

FATHER: I understand what you mean.

(*Rajan stares at him and Vimal goes into the house*)

But what is this case about Kajariwal ? I believe he was made to leave this room. Gaya Dutt came to our town a few days ago to inaugurate a school and he told me...All the firearms too have been sealed ?

RAJAN: I was deputed to this district to control the situation and I did it in the best way I could but Mr Kajariwal...

FATHER: He is very influential...

RAJAN: That is why he has not paid any income-tax for the last thirteen years. Every Collector who came here only added a few more sheets to the file.

(*He hands over the file to his father*)

I took action. It was my responsibility to recover the taxes.

FATHER: You should have done as the others had done.

(*Takes off his coat and tie*)

You too should have gone according to the times. Your sincerity and administrative ability are well known and I am proud of them but then it would be a folly to resign on such a mild and minor issue. Just think, how is the public going to react ?

RAJAN: I don't care.

FATHER: But I do. Your status, your living, your future...How about all of us ?

RAJAN: All of us ?

FATHER: I mean you should take it lightly. Don't worry.

RAJAN: (*Gets up*) To raise a man to be a Collector was your struggle; you have been a lawyer and a Collector was no less than God for you.

(*Vimal enters*)

VIMAL: Breakfast is ready.

FATHER: Come on, son. You should have your breakfast.

RAJAN: No thanks, I have finished. You get along. I've to wait for someone.

(*Vimal and Father go in and Rajan again gets busy with his files and papers. Sri enters the room*)

SRI: Mr Atman is here.

RAJAN: Ask him to wait for a while.

(*He is again busy with his papers. Vimal comes in*)

VIMAL: Why don't you join Father ?

RAJAN: You better do : it is enough.

VIMAL: Can't you give up your work even for a while?

(He does not answer and Vimal gets in again)

RAJAN: *(To Sri)* : Show him in.

(Atman enters)

Where is Mr Gaya Dutt ?

ATMAN: How do I know ?

RAJAN: I had asked for both of you together.

ATMAN: All is well, I hope.

RAJAN: I want to know what manipulations I did in the by-election ? Mr Atman, educated people like you shouldn't join such dirty politics.

ATMAN: You mean I should have joined the Administration ?

RAJAN: Well, politics has spoiled even administration.

ATMAN: Red-tapism is all we have learnt from the British. Bureaucracy has vitiated politics too...

RAJAN: Your politics also comes from the same system.

ATMAN: Well, it all comes from there: this politics, this administration, this feudal society—all have the same old origin.

RAJAN: The British are not there any longer.

ATMAN: The system remains the same. The same bureaucracy, the same red-tapism, vested interests, corruption in a modified shape...

RAJAN: Why don't you change the system? You're a popular labour leader; even then you lost to Gaya Dutt...Strange ?

ATMAN *(Laughter)* Well, it is all in the game. I've lost twice in the general elections and now in the by-election; have suffered imprisonment a number of times; tear-gas shells, lathi charges were all acceptable. The system remains where it was before, unchanged.

RAJAN: What does that mean ?

ATMAN: Everything has got rust on it now.
(*Pause*)

RAJAN: You've always been in the opposition.

ATMAN: And could never come out of that.
(*Laughter*)
The opponent is so powerful that we can't do a damn about it. He is extremely popular. He even conducts the opposition for us.

RAJAN: Aren't you ashamed ?
(*Atman laughs*)
Politics was basically a philosophy to improve the lot of the human race but it has become a short-cut to luxury, destroying man in every possible way.

ATMAN: What are you saying?

RAJAN: Everything loses its purpose.

ATMAN: That is history.

RAJAN: That is politics.

SRI: (*Intervening*) Mr Gaya Dutt is here.

RAJAN: Ask him to wait.
(*Sri walks out*)
Kajariwal has always taken advantage of the quarrel between you and Gaya Dutt. I want it to end.

ATMAN: We waste so much time in talking that we fail to differentiate between what we wish and what really happens.
(*Pause*)

RAJAN: There is no use talking to Gaya Dutt. Sri, tell him to see me some other time. I am busy at the moment.

GAYA DUTT: I am sorry for being late but then I have come. Actually some people had come and they had certain problems. How's your backache now?

RAJAN: I've got to talk to Mr Atman. It's serious.

GAYA DUTT: But I suppose, we too have certain things to talk about ?

RAJAN: Have a look at your watch, please.

GAYA DUTT: Forget about that.
(*Starts winding the watch*)
But now that I have come I suppose I will linger on.

ATMAN: He has a firm belief like the British. He is not going to leave.

GAYA DUTT: I believe your father is here. Where's he ? I've an old...
(*Laughter*)

ATMAN: (*Rising*) I think it is time for me to leave.

RAJAN: Are you going ?

GAYA DUTT: Well, he was hurt in a lathi charge some days ago. The doctor has advised him complete rest.

ATMAN: He knows everything. He only does not know about his death.
(*Atman laughs and then quietly leaves. Meanwhile, Sri has rearranged all the files on the office-table. He is now standing like a sentry*)

GAYA DUTT: I heard you're worried. I suppose the minister was not indifferent to you. I mean, these people speak a lot of nonsense, they are accustomed to such talk and it cannot be helped.
(*Rajan starts, continues to read the newspaper*)
I suppose the minister must have talked to you about Kajariwal ?
(*Rajan is indifferent; reading the newspaper*)
You're intelligent. In fact, you should not take the politicians seriously. You should avoid meeting them.
(*Rajan looks at him*)
He must have said something, didn't he ?

RAJAN: How are you concerned ?

GAYA DUTT: He telephoned the Chief Secretary in my presence.

RAJAN: Must have.

GAYA DUTT: I have great respect for you and I am under an obligation. I give you a fair suggestion: you better leave the case as it is and take charge of the new assignment.

RAJAN: Thanks a lot.

GAYA DUTT: Mr Kajariwal is a very good man. During the freedom struggle...

RAJAN: (*Putting aside the newspaper*) That's why he did not pay his income-tax all these years. The dues amount to nearly eight lakh sixteen thousand. The British Government allowed him to keep firearms without a licence. Is this his national struggle ?

(*He gets up as if he wanted to leave the room*)

GAYA DUTT: What's wrong in keeping firearms ? One keeps them only for prestige.

RAJAN: And does not pay taxes also because of prestige, I suppose ?

GAYA DUTT: Don't speak so loudly...Your father must be in the house. The General Manager of Kajariwal is waiting for him outside your bungalow.

RAJAN: I know all about it.

GAYA DUTT: I don't want to go to your superiors.

RAJAN: That is your privilege, your birth-right. For your kind information, your friend, Mr Kajariwal's godown must have been sealed by now.

GAYA DUTT: Too bad.

RAJAN: You cango now.

GAYA DUTT: Is it true ?

(*Pause*)

And if that is so, I suggest you withdraw your orders. It is in your interest.

RAJAN: That is impossible.

GAYA DUTT: Give it a thought.

RAJAN: Behave.

GAYA DUTT: All right.

RAJAN: This is your government and the decision of the cabinet is that the dues be collected. In a way I am executing your orders.

GAYA DUTT: Sir, you don't differentiate between order and desire.

(*Pause*)

What exactly do you want ?

RAJAN: How does that concern you ?

GAYA DUTT: In fact, I am your man whether you feel concerned or not.

RAJAN: Shut up...I don't need you or anyone else.

GAYA DUTT: You forget that you have entrusted everything to us.

RAJAN: And you have entrusted everything to us. We can foil all your plans by just concealing a particular file.

GAYA DUTT: I know that but even then you should seek our help.

(*Father appears at the door*)

GAYA DUTT: Well, nice to have met you. I was just enquiring about you. All well, I hope?

FATHER: Thank you. What've you people done here? You misinformed the minister about...

GAYA DUTT: You are an experienced lawyer. What I told the minister was in Mr Rajan's interest... After all, how could he get promotion, otherwise? Such tedious work and no name...How long could he remain just a Collector here ?

RAJAN: It would be better if both of you went out and discussed all these things.

GAYA DUTT: Come along, I will tell you.

(*Both of them walk out. Sri also quits the room*)

RAJAN: (*Dials a number*) Get me the Superintendent, please...Mr Rathor, what's the latest about the Harijan colony ? Yes, yes. Take strict measures. The Brahmins have got their colony burnt...no, no argument, please. Take everyone into police custody. (*Meanwhile Vimal has come to the room and sits on the sofa. Rajan dials again*) Hello, Mr A.D.M., did you go there ? Yes... that's right. I am typing the orders myself. No, I don't need a stenographer. I have spoken to Peshkar about it. I will be going there as soon as I finish the work here. No, I don't care for all that...yes...I have decided all about it.

(*Puts the receiver down*)

VIMAL: Mrs Rathor had telephoned. She wants to buy our car. We should also now go in for a new one.

RAJAN: Vimal, what preparation have you made till now ?

VIMAL: Thank God, you did say something.

RAJAN: Do you remember what I told you three days before our marriage? I told you that I would quit my job after the Collectorship.

VIMAL: You're talking of the days that have gone.

RAJAN: Well, actually I too had forgotten about it... I didn't know then in this profession there would be the same slavery and nothing else. To be sincere means your stepping into a quagmire from where you can never come out. I was not aware of this fraud. Now, tell me, what you have done about our leaving this place?

VIMAL: I have ?

RAJAN: Really ?

VIMAL: I've sent fees for both the children to be admitted into the convent hostel; have sold some old things to the property dealer for about Rs 4,500. And when we go there we shall add something to this money and buy a new model...

RAJAN: Go where ?

VIMAL: The place of your new posting.

RAJAN: Oh !

VIMAL: I have also told the insurance agent that we are taking out a new policy. I have also asked for the accounts from the bank.

RAJAN: I wasn't talking about this preparation. I was talking about getting out of...

VIMAL: Don't be childish.

RAJAN: Refrigerators, cars, insurance, status...

VIMAL: Then why did you get into this job ?

RAJAN: I had no choice.

VIMAL: What do you mean ?

RAJAN: Vimal...

VIMAL: Everyone has a false pretence. He wants to get out of it only to add to this false pretence. (*Rajan does not answer...the telephone rings*)
Hello...trunk call...from the Chief Secretary ...wait a second, please.

RAJAN: Good morning...yes sir. That is right, the godown has been sealed, firearms too...yes... yes sir. You will recall that I was given charge of this district...I have also got your secret orders. How could that be...how could I be like others? Your orders will be obeyed... no...no sir, I can't do that.
(*Puts the receiver down*)

VIMAL: We'll have to go the governmental way.

We should, at the same time, do our duty.

RAJAN: There is nothing new in that.

VIMAL: You need rest.

RAJAN: Yes...I will resign.

VIMAL: You've got to have a solid reason for that.

RAJAN: Determination...not reason.

VIMAL: Why do you want to resign all of a sudden? What would be the reaction ?

RAJAN: I don't have any enemy.

VIMAL: They come automatically, without any specific reason. That's the way of life.

RAJAN: You're talking like Father.

(*Vimal is quiet*)

One who has come in can also go out. I haven't been cruel to anyone. I have done no injustice. I've friends, home, family...I have everything one craves for.

VIMAL: The outsiders are there only because of our outer appearance.

RAJAN: Your thinking is narrow.

VIMAL: You don't care for anything. Didn't you notice how Father came desperately on hearing about your plan to resign?

RAJAN: I've explained it to him.

VIMAL: How are you going to tell it to your children?

RAJAN: They will continue their education in the house and will live like others.

VIMAL: What're you going to tell me?

RAJAN: You... ?

(*Silence*)

VIMAL: We had a love-marriage. You've no justification to make me live like that. All your friends, your relations have their children studying in convents. You've been a sincere, responsible and sensitive man...You had your principles ...And for that we...

(Walks into the house hurriedly. From the background one could hear the laughter shared by Gaya Dutt and Rajan's father. Slowly and gradually light fades from Rajan's face)

SCENE TWO

Same place
Evening of the same day

(*Empty stage. The telephone rings. Sri comes and picks up the receiver*)

SRI: Hello...Good morning, madam...I am sorry there is no one home at the moment...I will tell her when she is back...yes, certainly... why not...of course, madam.

(*Rajan enters from the right. Sri puts the receiver down*)

Mrs Rathor was on the line.

RAJAN: Will you tell Father to see me?

SRI: Sir, he is out to Kajariwal's party.

RAJAN: What ?

SRI: Kajariwal's driver was here at four in the afternoon.

RAJAN: Could you tell me if it was the same car in

which he came in the morning. Did you notice?

SRI: Yes sir, it was the same car.

RAJAN: Will you ask Vimal to come in?
(*Sits on the sofa*)

SRI: Sir, she is out to the market.

RAJAN: Was Vimal at home when Father went out?

SRI: Yes sir, she was at home.

RAJAN: Did she know where he was going?

SRI: I am not sure of that, sir.

RAJAN: Will you get me some water?
(*Sri goes into the house. Rajan gets up, reads some paper from the office-table, tears it off, rolls a new sheet on the typewriter and starts typing out something. Sri enters and keeps standing with a glass of water. Vimal enters from the left. She is holding some packets. Rajan takes the glass from Sri*)

VIMAL: I am terribly tired.
(*Relaxes on the sofa*)

RAJAN: (*Comes closer to her*) Where has Father gone?

VIMAL: Hasn't he returned yet?

RAJAN: But where has he gone?

VIMAL: Well, he has gone to Kajariwal's party.

RAJAN: Why did he go?
(*Vimal does not answer*)
How did he know that Father was here? His driver was here to collect him. Why didn't you inform me? Why should he go ?

VIMAL: How do I know?

RAJAN: How did Father come here, by train or... ?
(*Vimal is silent*)
He came in Kajariwal's car...Why didn't you tell me?
(*Pause*)

VIMAL: Father knows him well.

RAJAN: That means he is going to fight his case. But if he does that...

VIMAL: He said so.

RAJAN: Kajariwal has many lawyers like him in his clutches. I'm afraid he might not do something. Sri, get Kajariwal on the line.

(*Sri dials the number*)

Did you get it ?

SRI: Yes sir, the bell is ringing.

RAJAN: Ask for Father...

SRI: Hello...Is Mr Rajan's father there, please? Yes...

(*Aside*: *Sir, Kajariwal wants to speak to you*)

RAJAN: No, I am not interested. Ask for Father.

SRI (*Into the phone*): Hello...will you get Father on the line, please?

(*Aside* : *Sir, he wants to talk to you first*)

RAJAN: To me...?

(*Takes the receiver, makes an attempt to talk but then puts the receiver down*)

VIMAL: Father is not a fool to be cheated so very easily.

RAJAN: Well, I too was not a fool but see how Father got me into this. (*Pause*)

VIMAL (*Rising*): Sri, did Sahib have his tea ?

SRI: Not yet, madam.

(*Vimal moves to go in*)

RAJAN: I hope no bill is to be paid.

VIMAL: I had to clear only Sanval Das's account but then there was some miscalculation. Meanwhile, Mr Gaya Dutt came there all of a sudden and...

RAJAN: And he got the account set right.

VIMAL: What ?

RAJAN: Nonsense.

VIMAL: What's wrong with you ?

RAJAN: Show me that packet.
(*Takes it*)
Sanval Das...
(*Tears the packet off and takes out the saree, it gets loose and starts flowing*)
Sri, get me Sanval Das on the line.
(*Sri tries to locate the number. Meanwhile, Vimal goes off the stage*)
Tell him to come here and settle his account.

SRI: (*Into the phone*) Mr Sanval Das...This is Sri from the Collector's bungalow. Mr Rajan wants you to come here and settle your account...yes...well...
(*Aside : Sir, he says nothing is due*)

RAJAN: (*Takes the phone*) Forget about the settlement my wife made and come over with all the bills and take your payment.
(*Puts the receiver down*)
Who's there?

SRI: (*Looks out*) It is Father, sir.

RAJAN: Take this saree away.
(*Sri gathers the saree and puts it aside. Father enters from right*)
Father, where was the need to go there?

FATHER: I've known him for long and I deal with all his cases about his sugar mills.
(*Rajan is disturbed at this revelation, stares at him*)
Kajariwal is not that bad.

RAJAN: If you had to fight such cases, why did you bring me to this profession?

FATHER: Why don't you try to understand, my son?

RAJAN: What did he say?

FATHER: What was there to say?

RAJAN: What did you tell him?
(*Father laughs and Rajan gets disturbed*)
Father...?

FATHER: I am not foolish, my son.

RAJAN: Was anyone else present when you were talking to him?

FATHER: No, there was nothing but a tape-recorder which was playing music. He himself turned it off...

(Rajan is now greatly disturbed)

Son, it does not make any difference, the world is vast and ancient, there is no depth. We have to believe what the other person says. Man has made no progress. He has only been staging a drama of his success, mannerisms and various other things. In fact, he stands where he was...the same old fear, the same hunger, the same...

RAJAN: Do you remember what you talked to Kajariwal?

FATHER: You're unhappy because you remember everything. Forget about everything and be concerned with yourself. What right have we, what is our strength? We are not even a small part of this vast world...

RAJAN: Sri, take him in...

FATHER: Keep away.

(He goes into the house humming something. Rajan dials someone's number after a while)

RAJAN: Hello...yes...raid Mr Kajariwal's house immediately...do it in any way you like. There is something important in his tape-recorder... don't leave any tape there...get going immediately.

(Puts the receiver down, picks up a paper, tries to read it but cannot)

What am I ? It is time to ask myself. I could have told them earlier but was helpless because of my principles...what principles are they? It is nothing but an attempt to convince oneself of one's superiority. They say politics dragged the country to disaster... as if religion had done something less than that to bring us to this stage...

(*Vimal enters*)

VIMAL: Listen, listen...Father is saying something nonsensical to himself, he is talking to himself.

RAJAN: Religion has no answer to anything.

VIMAL: At least listen to what he is saying.

RAJAN: He's lucky.

VIMAL: Stop him.

RAJAN: He's my Father.

VIMAL: That does not mean anything.

RAJAN: I can't do anything about that.

VIMAL: What?

(*He does not answer*)

Why don't you ?

RAJAN: Something has got stuck in my throat... perhaps some principle and I am guarding it with mere words. Still I can't express myself...you can do that...Father can do it.

VIMAL: Rajan...?

(*He does not answer*)

SECOND ACT

Situation the same place
Time : the next day

(*The tape-recorder is playing music, conversation, noise and laughter alternatively. Rajan is listening to all this attentively. Vimal comes to the room and keeps standing behind Rajan, silently.*)

VIMAL: (*affectionately*) Hasn't it finished yet ?
(*he turns backward and embraces her*)
Put it off, now.
(*walks ahead and puts the switch off*)
Father wasn't willing to go today. He blessed me as I waited to touch his feet and said: "My dear daughter, everything is in your hands.
(*laughs*)
Oh, what's this ? You didn't shave today... ? What a bore
(*Rajan laughs it away...telephones rings*). *Vimal picks it up*)

Hello... Hello, Mrs Rathor, how are you ...I am fine...dinner party...certainly, by all means...Why don't you come over...let us settle it......definitely......come over...... (*puts the receiver down*)

RAJAN: Vimal, do you remember that small bungalow we lived in when I came in this service. One could enjoy the lovely landscape and natural beauty from the rear window. Do you remember how soothing it was to see the wimpling Ganges ?

VIMAL: You call that good ? There wasn't even enough place to accomodate things we got in marriage and we had to keep that in my father's house.

RAJAN: How pleasant it was to live in that room!

VIMAL: Yes, the dust from all around will come into the room...What a lovely room ?

RAJAN: It was really enjoyable to sleep there with the windows open.

VIMAL: And the mosquitoes made the sleep much more enjoyable... ?

RAJAN: I never liked sleeping with a mosquito-net.

VIMAL: You are a savage.

RAJAN: How is that ?

VIMAL: That forest-like environment...

RAJAN: That's how I was a savage and you a peahen. I would catch you anywhere and then we would be lost somewhere.

VIMAL: That was S.D.M.'s bungalow and this is D. M.'s. We've this front room where you have the office. We got to have one that suits our status.
(*pause*)

RAJAN: Each transfer brought us a better bungalow

and we naturally improved the environment.

VIMAL: There is a lot of difference between our first bungalow and one we are having now.

RAJAN: What are you trying to suggest?

VIMAL: Forget it...I am getting a sore throat.

RAJAN: We have been forgetting all that for which we created such an environment, such an atmosphere.

(*pause*)

Why do you wear such blouses now ?

VIMAL: Do you like it ?

RAJAN: You never put on such blouses in the past?

VIMAL: Well, you know, "necessity is the mother of invention."

RAJAN: That's to say it is not a blouse but an invention ?

(*they laugh together*)

See, how pleasant it is outside.

VIMAL: Let me change and we will go out.

RAJAN: Let us go as it is...right now...you look alright.

VIMAL: What would others think ?

RAJAN: What would anyone say ?

VIMAL: Have you ever seen Mrs Rathor going out... ?

RAJAN: You're Vimal and not Mrs Rathor...*you are the Vimal*, the one and only one.

VIMAL: You've even forgotten grammar. Don't you remember one should not use 'the' with proper noun. We should always be aware of people around.

RAJAN: That's why the usage...your hands are really very beautiful and it was with these very hands that you played the Sitar.

VIMAL: It is there in the living room...

RAJAN: And we have this environment too...Why don't you bring it and play those familiar tunes, those marvellous compositions.

VIMAL: At this hour... ?

RAJAN: What's wrong with the hour ?

VIMAL: Sometimes you talk like a child.

RAJAN: Well, take me for child at the moment. (*he takes her hand in his hand...Vimal laughs.. Rajan lets her hand go*)

VIMAL: You never let my hand go off so easily... our hands would tremble and you would take me into an affectionate embrace.

RAJAN: It was a different environment then.

VIMAL: But it was important for that.

RAJAN: Now get over it...we can't fill the gap with mere words.

VIMAL: But it was you who started it.

RAJAN: You're responsible for it.

VIMAL: But you are the basis.

RAJAN: That is ridiculous. I never desired this sort of atmosphere.

VIMAL: But you never reacted to it.

RAJAN: Vimal...

VIMAL: I am what you wanted me to be and ultimately these very things surrounded you...I did what you wanted me to do. I became what you wanted me to become. I put on the sort of clothes you wanted me to wear. I've always been moving according to your wishes without a word of complaint, without any objection whatsoever, without any choice and without a word, I did all that quietly.

RAJAN: But when did I...

VIMAL: Why didn't you...
(*silence*)
You've been the same from the day you en-

tered this profession. You've cared for nothing but your work.

RAJAN: Don't expect me to be like everyone else.

VIMAL: That's why it was necessary for me to have this kind of an environment, and I...

RAJAN: Vimal...

VIMAL: You think there is something else too that we haven't seen during all these years.

RAJAN: How and where... ?

VIMAL: Why didn't you see it?

RAJAN: This profession and you people have never let me come out of it. Someone ordered and my self-pride, my ego was provoked. Someone asked for me, someone saw, and someone...

VIMAL: Atman, Gaya Dutt, Kajariwal, father, and.. and myself...

RAJAN: What's this nonsense ?

VIMAL: You think all these people are there outside ?

RAJAN: You can't understand that.

VIMAL: Because I am not within.

RAJAN: How does it matter to you ?

(*she laughs*)

Atman, Gaya Dutt...

VIMAL: You would have been like one of them had you not come here.

RAJAN: Vimal...

VIMAL: I'm just being humorous.

RAJAN: Thanks a lot.

VIMAL: Come let's go out......or I will bring the Sitar......alright I will treat you like a child for a while.

RAJAN: Nice of you.

(*Vimal goes in. Rajan closes his eyes and the light*

falls only on him. Suddenly Atman appears in the surrounding darkness)

Is that you, Atman....

ATMAN: You've recognized me, after all?

RAJAN: I suppose so...

ATMAN: You want to get out of the system ?

RAJAN: Positively !

ATMAN: Let's do that.

RAJAN: Is there a way out ?

ATMAN: It is never there, one has to create it.

RAJAN: One has to create it....why do people stare at me ?

ATMAN: Why should that disturb you ?

RAJAN: But they are not unknown, they are our own people.

ATMAN: They are only too selfish.

RAJAN: I love them.

ATMAN: Anyway, step out now.

RAJAN: How to do that ?

ATMAN: I will demonstrate

(*shows him how to take a step further, it does not involve any special way but just the ordinary way of walking*)

Do you get me ?

RAJAN: That's fine but where should I put it ?

ATMAN: On the ground, where else.

RAJAN: But how about the gap between the step and the ground ?

(*Atman laughs*)

You laugh at that. You don't know me well, do you ?

ATMAN: How could I do that? I joined politics and you came into Administration ..You then got busy with your domestic life, worked day and night and I got into the opposition... Saw you a couple of times in the way but you always evaded me. I even waved at you a number of times. A number of times..

RAJAN: I have seen you often...busy in a public speech, some heated arguments about one thing or the other, leading some demonstration...Violating Section 144 (PC)...Signing the nomination papers in front of me...and at the forfiture of the election security money.

ATMAN: Is this your awakening...you forget the struggle for freedom starts only after independence.

RAJAN: I am aware of this, I am aware of the awakening...

ATMAN: That is nonsense ..I've nothing to do with you now...It is 14 years...14 years ago we separated never to meet again like the two ends of the sea....

RAJAN: But I am alone.

ATMAN: No place remains vacant for long...some stranger must have filled the gap.

RAJAN: What is this nonsense ?

ATMAN: You want an excuse to get away from here.. all right, take this revolver and kill me.

RAJAN: (*terrified*) You want to commit suicide ?

ATMAN: There is, in this world, no other way of overcoming the problems.

RAJAN: Is this where you want to take me ?

(*in the same darkness now appears Gaya Dutt from the other side of the stage*)

GAYA DUTT: But is this not within you?

RAJAN: I am safe here.

ATMAN: But I am not.

RAJAN: This is not my responsibility.

GAYA DUTT: Not mine, either.

ATMAN: It is not even mine.

RAJAN: Why did you let it be so ?

GAYA DUTT: Why did you ?

ATMAN: Who has got power ?

RAJAN: You had it..you are free.

GAYA DUTT: You were a high official.

ATMAN: And you a successful politician.

(*both Atman and Gaya Dutt speak the next dialogue together*)

That is right, perfectly all right. Our aim is to be superior to one another on the basis of personal authority and influence. That is how we are poles apart, so indifferent to one another.

RAJAN: Why did you ?

GAYA DUTT: (*to Rajan*) You did not cooperate with me..

ATMAN: (*to Rajan*) You betrayed me..you let me go into his hands, blindly.

GAYA DUTT: I fought a lone battle.

RAJAN: So did I, day and night.

(*Atman and Gaya Dutt answer that jointly*)

To keep the system going ?

RAJAN: No.

GAYA DUTT: Who has more power, tell me ?

RAJAN: You have.

GAYA DUTT: No, you have that.

(*Atman and Gaya Dutt together*)

Only you have that.

GAYA DUTT: You want to get out of here all alone, leaving us. Do you know what will you find outside...me, only me.

ATMAN: I am there too.

(*Rajan closes his eyes again in fear.. Atman and Gaya Dutt disappear in the dark.. Rajan walks out quickly after which there is complete darkness on the stage for a while. Vimal enters the room at the fading-in of the lights...she is, it looks, trying to find someone*)

VIMAL: Mrs Rathor...Mrs Rathor...Where are you ?

MRS RATHOR: It is an interesting magazine. You too seem to be terribly interested in Hindi films...Look at this here...where did it come from...astonishing.

VIMAL: I mostly see English films.

(*silence......a voice from the background...Vimal... Vimal...*)

I am coming, father.

MRS RATHOR: When did your father-in-law come ?

VIMAL: This afternoon.

(*she goes in ..Mrs Rathor starts humming a film tune while looking through the magazine. Vimal enters*)

MRS RATHOR: Whom have you fixed for dinner arrangements tomorrow.

VIMAL: Father feels we should fix a good caterer. He wants that..

MRS RATHOR: How about Mr Rajan, what does he think of it ?

VIMAL: Mr Rajan...?

(*laughs*)

There is nothing for him to think...everything has been calculated quietly......no leakout anywhere.

MRS RATHOR: How could that be. I will tell him in such a way that.. (*she laughs*).

VIMAL: I suppose *buffet* system is ideal these days.

MRS RATHOR: I do think so because one can have his choice ...one can stand, sit, relax anywhere one likes.

VIMAL: One also gets an opportunity to see and show...

MRS RATHOR: Move around and talk to anyone, the choice remains with the person.

VIMAL: And if one does not want to talk to anyone he or she can sit quietly aloof (*laughter from both*).

MRS RATHOR: And to fill the silence play on the plate with spoon, make sound...

(joint laughter again)

VIMAL: To my mind, we speak at parties only because we don't want to talk to others.

(pause)

MRS RATHOR: Where is your ayah ?

VIMAL: Dismissed her.. she had started flirting with the driver.

MRS RATHOR: These ayahs are a big nuisance.

VIMAL: Where have you got your hair set ?

MRS RATHOR: Nowhere...I've myself done it...this is not bad, I hope.

VIMAL: I used to do similarly but my present hair-set is the one in vogue now...that is somewhat outdated.

MRS RATHOR: You are mistaken, it is back is fashion. There is something unique about it...it brings a certain distinctive quality to one's appearance.

(a pause)

VIMAL: Do you like my car... ?

MRS RATHOR: I do...but I think we will go in for a latest model...

VIMAL: Yes, that is true....I think we should maintain two cars now. Moreover, this is lucky for us...

(a momentary pause)

MRS RATHOR: Mr Rathor is also getting promotion. In fact, he would have had it long back if he had cared to. The Inspector-General is my uncle's first cousin.

VIMAL: In the real sense, Mr Rajan's promotion has just started ...one only needs to start once...

(silence)

VIMAL: Don't you have a cooking-range ?

MRS RATHOR: Well, we don't like bread made on it.

VIMAL: We have so many valuable things in store that it is a problem to pack everything.

MRS RATHOR: We don't buy useless things.

VIMAL: Innocence is your privilege...!

MRS RATHOR: One should not be so rude, Mrs Rajan.

VIMAL: You forced me.

MRS RATHOR: You are responsible for that.

VIMAL: Not me...It is you.

MRS RATHOR: No, it is you.

(Rajan enters the stage with Atman from the right wing. The ladies are quiet...give a pretended display of pleasure.

RAJAN: *(entering)* Is it possible that Kajariwal should lock-out his mill like that.

ATMAN: Nothing is impossible with him.

RAJAN: I have summoned him in the court.

ATMAN: It makes no difference to him.

RAJAN: It will...I will show him the difference before going.

VIMAL: *(to Mrs Rathor)* Do you hear him... ?

MRS RATHOR: Even Mr Rathor sometimes talks like that.

VIMAL: There is a big difference between the two.

ATMAN: I feel nothing is going to happen.

RAJAN: Did you enter politics with this belief ?

ATMAN: No, politics has brought on me this belief.

RAJAN: *(suddenly)* Oh, I am sorry, Mrs Rathor.

MRS RATHOR: Thank God, you got time for that. How are you ?

RAJAN: How *are* you *(stressing on 'are')*

MRS RATHOR: You've a grand dinner at your place tomorrow.

RAJAN: A grand dinner ?

MRS RATHOR: A farewell dinner...a dinner to celebrate your new assignment.

RAJAN: What nonsense is this ?

VIMAL: You think this is nonsense... ?

MRS RATHOR: *(smilingly and intimately)* But I've arranged

this dinner.

(*silence*)

RAJAN: This is not just a dinner...thi' is making fun of me.

MRS RATHOR: What do you mean ?

VIMAL: Let him say.

RAJAN: I am not just going to talk....I'll show it in action.

(*meanwhile Atman walks across the book-shelf and picks up a book, gets absorbed in it*)

ATMAN: Where will you go...after resigning.

RAJAN: Out of the system.

ATMAN: What would be the next step ?

(*starts playing the musical toy*)

RAJAN: I don't intend forming a party like you.

ATMAN: It is not a question of desiring nor rejecting. There again something happens suddenly, automatically.

RAJAN: I hate politics.

ATMAN: Hear...Hear...That's what he too wanted.

(*Rajan walks out briskly*)

VIMAL: Excuse me, I will be with you in a while.

(*she goes in*)

MRS RATHOR: (*to Atman*) I think I have seen you somewhere.

ATMAN: In police custody... ?

MRS RATHOR: I believe you are a good speaker.

ATMAN: I...? You are mistaken...That is Mr Gaya Dutt.

MRS RATHOR: Oh, I am sorry. I thought you are Gaya Dutt.

ATMAN: Thank you for the compliment...whatever it may mean.

(*pause*)

MRS RATHOR: You are a big labour leader, why don't you start some kind of a revolution ?

ATMAN: Revolution....In fact, I feel, one has to come to see man not as a free, but as a determined human-being. Not as a mover, but one to be moved. He is like a blind fungus.... a cosmic waste of matter.

MRS RATHOR: You speak excellent English. I have been looking for a good English tutor.

(*Atman is astonished*)

I am sure you are free these days...you should get full-pay leave before elections...I love English...

(*Atman leaves out of disguest. Vimal and Rajan appear from inside*)

VIMAL: After all he is your father.

RAJAN: All around there is something or the other... What am 'I' then ?

(*silence*)

VIMAL: Has Mr Atman left... ?

MRS RATHOR: My God, how good he is at English.

(*silence...telephone rings*)

VIMAL: Hello...from the court...(to Rajan)...Here, A.D.M. is on line.

RAJAN: Yes...what...?...Impossible...What has 'Stay-order' got to do in Kajariwal case.... Yes...Send the file and the orders to me... immediately.

(*puts the receiver down*)

VIMAL: It is an official case and it is for the government to do what it wants. For an official nothing is personal.

RAJAN: (*hurt*) The slave has no individuality !

VIMAL: Why do you feel about it?

RAJAN: Even man is a product or object for you.

VIMAL: Why do you bring everything to the same point?

RAJAN: That is the central point.

VIMAL: It is difficult to argue with you, as if you are the Government.

RAJAN: I am nothing and I want to start my new life from here... (silence). There would be no dinner here.

MRS RATHOR: What is so unusual about it ? Mr Rathor has to encounter such situations quite frequently.

VIMAL: There is a difference between the two.

(*father enters the stage from inside*)

FATHER: What's wrong, Vimal ?

VIMAL: Some 'Stay Order' has come in Kajariwal case.

MRS RATHOR: Hello...come and have a seat here.. I will make a move now...give me a ring...okay... bye...bye.

(*quits from the left wing*)

FATHER: What can anyone do about it ?

RAJAN: Man can do everything.

(*silence*)

VIMAL: He says, there would be no dinner here.

(*father nods*)

VIMAL: We have been to several dinners, we too will have to throw in one.

RAJAN: I will apologize.

VIMAL: How will I?

FATHER: The point is...

RAJAN: Please, for heaven's sake, let it be so.

(*father and Vimal go into the house. Sri brings the file and goes out, Rajan looks through it. Sri again appears*)

GAYA DUTT: You rascal...Are you in senses ?

(*enters the room*)

What system is this ?

RAJAN: Will you mind sitting there... ?

(*indicating towards the corner chair*)

GAYA DUTT: So very kind of you..it is somewhat oppressive inside the room today..why shouldn't we go out for a stroll ?

(*Gaya Dutt is standing near the office table while*

Rajan is absorbed in some documents)

Looks like the 'Stay Order'. The court has granted a 'Stay' to Kajariwal on the grounds that the tax assessment is without jurisdiction. And an action will be taken against him only when the charge is proved. He is undergoing a big loss because his godown has been sealed What could one do, everything goes..

RAJAN: Please don't disturb me.

GAYA DUTT: Is there anything I could do for you? The house looks somewhat isolated without children..I hear your father is here..he is an excellent man..I have known him...

RAJAN: What help did I render during the by-election ?

GAYA DUTT: Oh ! Forget about that..

RAJAN: You will have to tell me..

GAYA DUTT: You have been such an efficient and responsible officer..

(*Rajan is astonished*)

One must keep some good officials along. When I go to the 'Centre', I will take you along.

RAJAN: You will have to pay a penalty for that.

GAYA DUTT: You can't file a petition against me now, the time for that is over.

RAJAN: I have other ways of doing that.

GAYA DUTT: You think I have been doing nothing about that.

RAJAN: You are not aware of my powers.

GAYA DUTT: That is precisely what I do—keeping a track of other people's powers. That is politics. Is there any philosophy behind that ?

(*laughs*) I understand you are going to quit this job. Remember, I will see to it that enquiries are instituted against you. And all the allegations will be proved, there are thousands of us who will stand witness against you.

RAJAN: There would be more of them with me than you.

GAYA DUTT: (*a laughter*) Poor chap ! The educated elite will either work or be with us. What does it mean to come out is beyond your comprehension, anyway. You, while you are in job, can't forgo these comforts and luxuries even for a moment.

RAJAN: You are underestimating me.

GAYA DUTT: I am well aware of your status and position but I can prove that you used unfair means during the by-election.

(*pin-drop silence*)

Come on, get up, pick up the receiver, come on, what are you so hesitant about ?

RAJAN: (*shouting*) Shut..up..

(*there should be a pause, very small one between shut and up. After this shouting Rajan picks up the receiver*).

Yes..Rajan here..yes..yes, the seal from Kajariwal's godown should be removed and the firearms be returned.

(*puts the receiver down*)

GAYA DUTT: Sir, we too have some problems..remember me if there is anything I could do for you.. goodbye then.

(*Gaya Dutt quickly walks out and Rajan starts typing something. Vimal appears from the inner door*)

VIMAL: Come in..tea has been served and father is waiting for you..What is this ?..Resignation......!

RAJAN: Will you bring my 'Will' from the safe ?

VIMAL: The key is with you...

RAJAN: What?

VIMAL: I don't know the whereabouts of the key ever since you locked your *will* in that. (*pause*) But my jewellery is in bank lockers.

RAJAN: You are not concerned about my 'Will'?

VIMAL: Your tea is getting cold.

RAJAN: Thanks..

(*Father appears from the inner door*)

FATHER: Come, let's have tea. This hard work day and night...

RAJAN: This is what you wanted.

FATHER: Only I wished that..?

RAJAN: Who else..?

FATHER: One shouldn't think in those terms.

RAJAN: It would have been marvellous.

FATHER: What other problem have you now ?

RAJAN: You are a lawyer..I am merely a *case* for you.

FATHER: This is what you think ?

RAJAN: But why do I ?

(*Atman rapidly walks in from outside*)

ATMAN: (*to Rajan*) You wanted evidence against both of them..here it is..Kajariwal had offered me the post of 'Honorary Labour Adviser', most confidentially, on a salary of three thousand rupees a month. And this is Gaya Dutt's great act..this secret letter which he had given to one of his close associates for my murder. It was just a matter of chance that the man happened to be a friend of the Union members.

(*Rajan could not get hold of the letters..one is in father's hands while Vimal has got hold of the other one*)

FATHER: One can file an excellent suit against him.

VIMAL: One could arrest Gaya Dutt on the basis of this.

FATHER: Do you have any other such documents with you ?

VIMAL: I am sure you must be having many more of them.

RAJAN: (*suddenly*) Who is it ? Who's there ?
(*Gaya Dutt enters*)
Didn't you go ?

GAYA DUTT: I was talking to some of your policemen.. they too have a lot of grievances. Well, Mr Atman what have you brought. ?

RAJAN: Mr Atman, please go to the police station..

GAYA DUTT: Oh, he has brought some letters. Mr Atman what has Mr Rajan got to do with your personal letters ?

ATMAN: I don't want to talk to you.

GAYA DUTT: I am only worried about you. I have a great regard for you. For instance, you are an excellent speaker. Our society is proud of you.

ATMAN: (*taking both letters*) Anyway, I can't surrender to this gangsterism...

GAYA DUTT: Mind your language, at least. You should know where you are.

ATMAN: (*sarcastically*) Between the two of you.. gangsterism and bureaucracy.

FATHER: (*in anger*) You two may go out and fight.

RAJAN: Is that all ? So soon..it has got on your nerves.

VIMAL: Come father, let us go in.
(*they both go out*)

GAYA DUTT: Give me the letters.

ATMAN: I will get them published and tell people how shallow and corrupt is our democracy which depends on bureaucracy. This is a new socialism which will give birth to a new Fascism.

GAYA DUTT: Cheers..cheers. Excellent ideas. Can you stop it ?

ATMAN: I only know one thing, the walls of society that all of you have built up will have to be demolished before anything new and positive could be done.

GAYA DUTT: You are a destroyer..you have no constructive power.

ATMAN: The very source of construction has been badly obstructed by black mountains like you.

GAYA DUTT: Stop this nonsense.

ATMAN: This shapeless and struck insipid non-entity might destroy me but I can't stand his ominous face any longer.

GAYA DUTT: Stop..where are you going ?

(*Gaya Dutt follows Atman going out. A few moments later a bullet-shot is heard from the background. Vimal and father come rushing in from inside the bungalow*)

FATHER: What has happened ?

VIMAL: Why don't you speak ?

FATHER: What has happened ?

(*they both run out...Gaya Dutt enters the stage*)

GAYA DUTT: Too bad..Atman has committed suicide.

RAJAN: You have killed Atman..I am an eye-witness.

GAYA DUTT: Outside the boundary of your...

RAJAN: You have killed..

GAYA DUTT: You won't escape either.

(*Gaya Dutt quickly quits the stage. Vimal comes running from the other end*)

VIMAL: My God ? who has killed Atman like that ?

RAJAN: I have killed him..he didn't even cry.

VIMAL: Stop this nonsense.

RAJAN: I can go out of this system now.

VIMAL: Yes, you will be hanged.

RAJAN: I will be hanged... (*laughs*)

VIMAL: How silly ?

RAJAN: (*as if in the court-room*) I have killed him intentionally, in all consciousness. He was innocent..innocent from his birth..ignorant, helpless..he was made what others wanted to make of him (*suddenly*)..No, that is wrong.. he was really guilty. He was of the belief that man is free to the extent that he could commit suicide. He is independent to bear all injustice, sin..to know the crime and go insane with arguments.

(*Gaya Dutt and father enter the stage in hurry*)

GAYA DUTT: Listen, Mr Rajan..listen..quick..

VIMAL: (*panic-struck intervenes*) It so happened..it so happened that..in fact, the whole thing is that Mr Atman was in great anger I don't know why. He was abusing everyone. He was abusing you, Mr Rajan and practically everyone...vulgar abuses. You know, we have to give charge tomorrow and leave. How are we concerned with the world? We have to walk our way almost blindly. Rs 2,500 is the basic salary of a Commissioner while he has to reach at least the status of a Secretary and will retire at a salary of at least Rs 3,500. By that time our Provident Fund will be nearly two and a half lakh. He will get nearly Rs 1,000 as pension and, you know, no one sits at home after retiring. He will be an Executive Director in some firm, or a Finance Adviser of some and if not that a Vice-chancellor of some University...

(*During this discourse Gaya Dutt tries several times to speak and stop Vimal in-between. On the other side the telephone bell after ringing for sometime automatically stops. By this time Vimal is almost breathless, having spoken for so long*)

GAYA DUTT: What nonsense is this, we don't have time now.

VIMAL: No, no, please listen to me, please let me finish.

GAYA DUTT: (*harshly*) You please keep quiet..
(*silence*)
(*to father*) What do you say, is this not a suicide case..?

FATHER: Yes, the place where the bullet has struck, falling obversely and the revolver lying near the right hand are enough of evidence.

GAYA DUTT: The policeman on duty outside is an eye-witness.

FATHER: Not saying a word, not crying or calling for help prove the point further.

RAJAN: (shouting) Yes, he has committed suicide.
(*walks out hurriedly in desperation, father and Gaya Dutt follow him*)

VIMAL: (*happily*) Oh, it is terribly hot.
(*lights fade out..after a few moments dim light fades in..a tape-recorder is playing..Rajan is on a sofa with a file and some papers in front. Suddenly strange noises come out of the tape-recorder—Rajan stops the machine abruptly*)

RAJAN: Who is it ?....Who are you ?...Where were you hiding...Within me !..for fourteen years since I took up this job...you thief, scoundrel. One needs a lot of self-confidence to act on something...Who are you facing...Myself... talkative...yes...don't try to dirty my room, stop, beware, don't touch my papers...don't touch the chair...don't try to misplace anything in the room...you can't change the balance of the room....Look at this photograph (cross marks with a chalk-piece a hanging photograph...Is that a statue...Is it necessary that a broken statue be there for decoration...How much had to be spent... how could that be remembered....Get out... shut up......only truth can save you now and nothing else...no one else...keep quiet you rascal...this is what people will say of you...I will kill you...you will not be able to say anything further...get out of here...only you were trying to search for something.. in this...in this...in that...

(*the file is thrown, papers are flown in the air*)

how could you do that, you senseless...having lost, why enact this drama of struggle. You have nothing to do with Atman. You had left him the moment you got in here...... then I was born. Atman, Gaya Dutt, Rajan, Kajariwal—you have formed a sort of trap around yourself...I have been fighting all-along...The same lost battle...I have been working honestly...You have been honestly trying to keep up the system...That was all in my powers...Why didn't you come out of it then...I am a responsible person...Not *person*, only responsible (*laughs*) a talented and sagacious person is special in everything, special even in his service...I have never done any injustice...You only did injustice to yourself...Day and night I was absorbed in my work...But never let yourself in into anything. Saved something everytime for this day. But it never happens, nothing like this happens...Listen...Listen...I have listened a lot. For the self defence so many arguments, so many principles...How can you say that...Yes, you did a lot of justice only to hide injustice. You punished the criminal only to hide the crime, to cover the crimes. Committed suicide only to keep yourself alive.

(*Rajan tries to sit on a sofa*)

Then you had the idea that after independence the struggle for freedom starts...That is there even now...With my birth a new confidence took birth in you. There are only two ideas in modern society : service and politics...Will you get out of my way...Whatever has happened in your time is your responsibility..That is absolutely wrong . .You have known nothing but yourself. What happened all these years, you have only got this tape.

(*plays the recorder, strange noises, voices, cries and shoutings emerge from it. Rajan stops the machine*)

You can stop that but how will you erase what has been recorded on me. Look here, there are immense tracks....

(*starts the machine again and himself goes on speaking something in a strange language. Unable to bear this Rajan falls flat on the floor*)

Get up, come here, sit here. Take this resignation note of yours and tear if off. You have lost this case, you will have to admit. Hold this 'Charge Certificate' and fill it up, sign on it.

(*Rajan is going to do that. Slowly fading of the lights, absolute darkness. After a while lights fade in again, well lighted stage and soft music could be heard. Father is talking to various guests while Vimal is busy discussing something with Mrs Rathor*)

MRS RATHOR: (*to Vimal*) You look gracious in this saree.

VIMAL: Where do you get your blouses stitched ?

(*on the other side*)

GAYA DUTT: See, people talk of freedom, independence but they do not know that man is getting down and down, like the roots of a tree.

FATHER: But the roots go deep into the soil and darkness only for their feed.

VOICES: That is true, yes...exactly.

A MAN: Isn't there any good film coming in the near future.

A WOMAN: "The Flying Saucer"...it has just been released.

VOICES : "The Flying Saucer".

(*they laugh*)

VIMAL: I have dismissed that ayah because she could not speak English...

MRS RATHOR: How much do you weigh these days ?

GAYA DUTT: (to father) Sir, I don't have time otherwise...

FATHER: That is true...It is already time for dinner.

A MAN: I think Mr Atman was not a man of politics. (*addressing another*) Have you ever heard of a politician commtting suicide ?

(*A gentleman walks into the room with his wife*)

FATHER: Hello...come along...

GAYA DUTT: Hello, how are you Mr Puri ? Not seen for quite some time. Is she your wife ? What is your name, young lady. (*the woman does not like that*). Why don't you come this way, the ladies are in that corner.

THE MAN: I had come to see Mr Rajan.

FATHER: He should be here any moment. Why don't you have a seat.

GAYA DUTT: (*to someone*) We have no dearth of beauty in this country. Leave apart woman, even plants, trees, animals and birds are exceedingly beautiful ..*Bande Mataram.*

FATHER: That's right.

GAYA DUTT: What is this arrangement ?

FATHER: Vimal, will you see what's the delay ?

VIMAL: Why don't you all go in, everything is ready ?

GAYA DUTT: Sir, I do nothing secretly.

VIMAL: Sri, bring the stuff here.

GAYA DUTT: Bring a larger one. Do you get me ? ...Yes, what was I talking about...?

A MAN: You were talking about beauty.

GAYA DUTT: Yes, I remember that now. It all depends on the country's climate. Am I wrong ?

ANOTHER MAN: How could you be ?

GAYA DUTT: On the whole Atman was a nice fellow. The only trouble with him was that he was talking in terms of basic change. Now how could that be...

(*Sri enters with a tray with drinks*)

FATHER: Don't forget this is the third you are having. The doctor has advised you against it. You have to do a lot yet for the country.

A MAN: The country expects a lot from you.

ANOTHER MAN: May God give you a long life.

A MAN: And a healthy long life.

GAYA DUTT: Look, who works in this country except the officers and the high-ups in administration.

MRS RATHOR: Now look at that: Mr Rathor hasn't turned up yet. In fact, he is an extremely busy person.

VIMAL: Take care of the arrangements, too.

GAYA DUTT: Where is Mr Rajan ? He should be here. So many people have come to meet him.

FATHER: He must be on his way.

A MAN: We haven't come across a better officer in this district before.

GAYA DUTT: You have said the right thing. Stupendous !

FATHER: This is all due to the good wishes of all of you.

GAYA DUTT: He has a very bright future.

(*women break into laughter at something, on the other side of the room*)

GAYA DUTT: We should also laugh..Ha..ha..ha..haa

(*other people also join him*)

(*Rajan enters the stage with remarkable gusto and dignity. People present greet him in various ways: 'please accept our congratulations', 'Congratulations', 'Bravo' and so on. He has been surrounded by the entire horde. He gets away from there and comes towards the sofa. People have surrounded him badly, almost trapped with the chain of people, Rajan, amidst the whole lot, is trying to say something but his voice is lost in the noisy atmosphere. Once again people start moving from one corner of the room to the other, forming their own groupings. And amongst them all, Rajan stands alone and quiet, mute and motionless*)

GAYA DUTT: Now just see the time, Mr Kajariwal hasn't turned up yet, though his gift has reached.

(*Gaya Dutt gulps the remaining drink in one drought and the spittings come to Rajan's face*)

RAJAN: What is this stupidity, this is unbearable. I belong to you all but that does not mean...

(*Having said so Rajan becomes a part of the crowd. Almost everyone is talking, unconcerned about the others. The atmosphere is tense with strange noises, conversation, arguments. These voices mixed with the soft pre-dinner music makes the situation unbearable for Rajan. He is no longer a part of the horde of people. He is there alone and quiet, no one is looking at him. To get busy Rajan gets absorbed in a telephone conversation. Vimal walks towards him and adjusts herself beside him...*)

CURTAIN